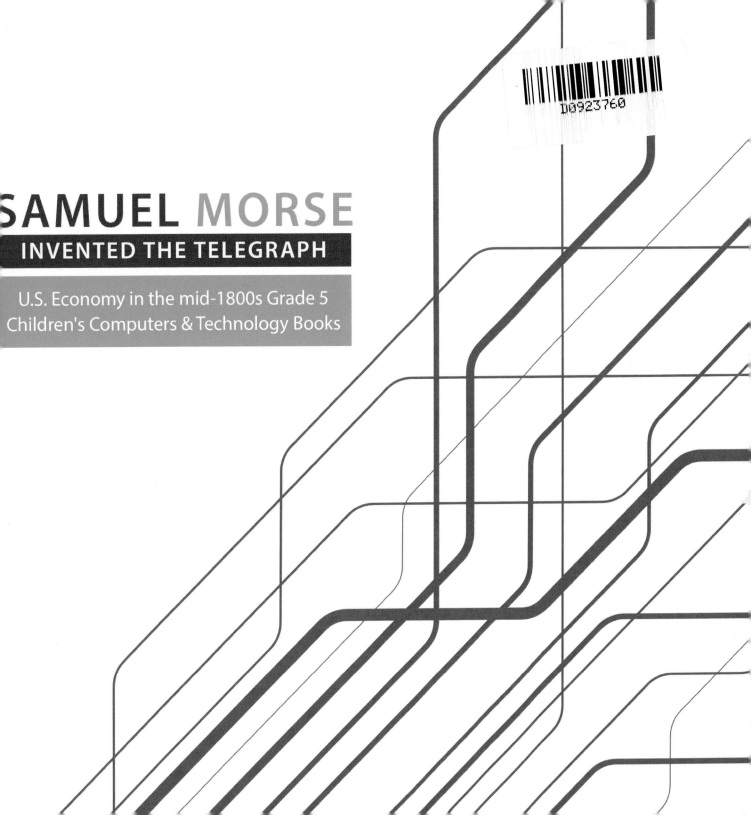

SAMUEL MORSE

INVENTED THE TELEGRAPH

U.S. Economy in the mid-1800s Grade 5
Children's Computers & Technology Books

Tech Tron
Computers & Technology

First Edition, 2020

Published in the United States by Speedy Publishing LLC, 40 E Main Street, Newark, Delaware 19711 USA.

© 2020 Tech Tron Books, an imprint of Speedy Publishing LLC

Tech Tron Books are available at special discounts when purchased in bulk for industrial and sales-promotional use. For details contact our Special Sales Team at Speedy Publishing LLC, 40 E Main Street, Newark, Delaware 19711 USA. Telephone (888) 248-4521 Fax: (210) 519-4043. www.speedybookstore.com

10 9 8 7 6 * 5 4 3 2 1

Print Edition: 9781541960466
Digital Edition: 9781541963467

See the world in pictures. Build your knowledge in style.
www.speedypublishing.com

TABLE OF CONTENTS

CAPITALISM AND THE UNITED STATES ECONOMY

The United States of America (USA) has an economy that is based on a system by the name of capitalism. In this economic system, it is not the government that owns and operates companies. Instead, companies are owned and run by private citizens themselves.

Business enterprise companies

It is the people who are in charge of the type of products that are manufactured and what type of services are delivered. Company owners have the freedom to determine the price of their goods and/or services.

Business owner leading informal in-house business meeting

Free enterprise and free-market economy are sometimes used to describe capitalism. Capitalist is the term given to a person who invests his/her own money into a company and operates it for the purpose of making a profit.

A BRIEF HISTORY OF THE ECONOMY IN THE UNITED STATES IN THE 1800S

Both lifestyles and the economy were different in the United States in the 1800s than they are today. Many people were farmers.

Farming was a popular way of life in the US during the 1800s

They grew their own food, had their own livestock and eked out a survival through self-sufficiency.

New Jersey farmhouse, 1800s

People building their own homes

They built their own homes from homemade tools and filled their homes with homemade furniture. In addition, they made their own clothes.

During the mid 1800s, farmers began to trade their produce with other farmers. When a season yielded a surplus crop, farmers took the extra crops and traded them for crops that were grown on other farms.

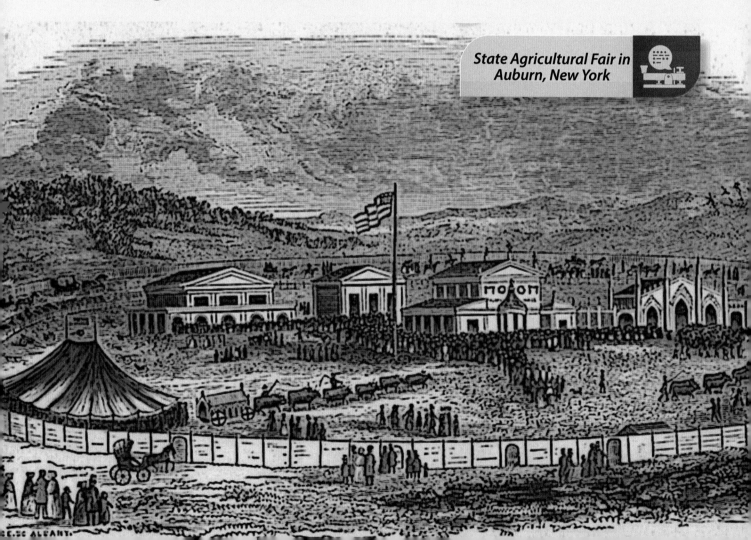

State Agricultural Fair in Auburn, New York

Eventually, farmers started to focus on the growth of one or more types of crops. They realized that crop specialization could result in economic gain.

Reaping wheat by hand in the early 1800s near Syracuse, NY

Before long, farms started to develop into industries in which a lot of different products were grown and sold for profit. In addition to changes in farming, other areas of industry started to undergo change in terms of specialization.

Farmers pressing apples to make cider in the 1800s

THE INDUSTRIAL
REVOLUTION

Milling machine, Massachusetts, New England, USA

During this period of U.S. history, most people inhabited the Northeast part of the country. As a natural result of this population concentration, the area is also where the industrial hub of the country took place.

People wanted to be in control of the production and trade of their own goods.

Cotton plantation on the Mississippi River

Companies started to build factories through which the manufacturing of goods could be made en masse.

Portsmouth Shoe Company, Portsmouth, New Hampshire, USA

First when factories and industries started to become popular, they appeared in areas that boasted a large population so that workers could easily be hired.

New England Factory life, USA

The factories and industries were also strategically located near water sources, such as rivers, so that goods could easily be shipped.

New Jersey Steel and Iron Works factory in Trenton, New Jersey

Sewing machines were invented during the first Industrial Revolution to decrease the amount of manual sewing work performed in clothing companies

Moreover, new machinery was being invented and these machines helped to increase manufacturing and production levels. A couple of machines in particular, the sewing machine, and the reaper were of great importance.

In addition, the use of rubber and other materials opened the doors for the production of specific types of products.

Rubber Mill

The use of factories resulted in the rapid production of goods at a low cost. Business owners were able to acquire a lot of wealth from the selling of their goods.

Steel factories at night near Pittsburgh, Pennsylvania

However, many of the people who worked in the factories were women and children. The pay which they received for the work was quite low.

A woman and a child working in a factory, North Carolina

Nonetheless, newcomers still came to the United States to work and to increase their quality of life. At this time, there was an increase in the number of people living in urban areas as opposed to those who remained in rural areas.

Mulberry Street, on the Lower East Side, New York

With the construction of the Transcontinental Railroad, migration westward increased.

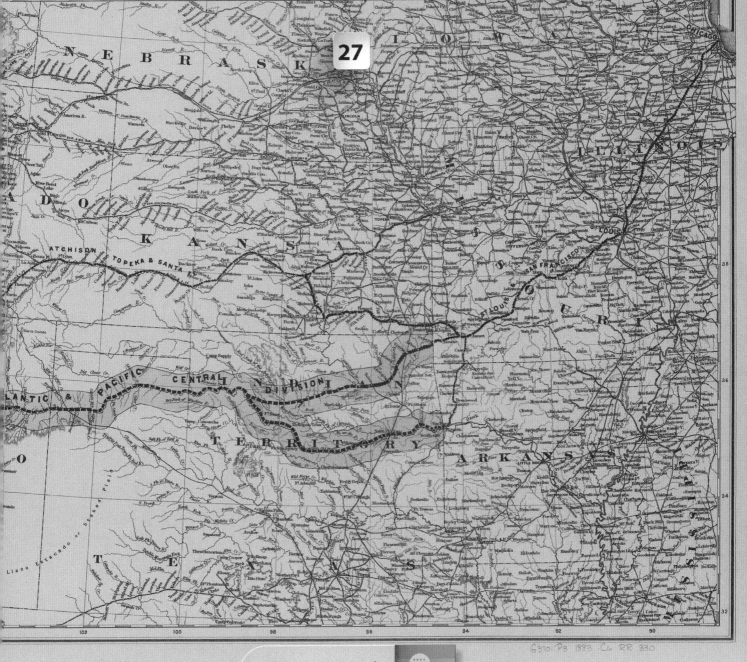

Transcontinental railroad route

People started to take an interest in the west part of the country. Industries, factories and businesses were being expanded.

Joining the tracks for the first transcontinental railroad, Promontory, Utah, 1869

SAMUEL MORSE AND THE ARRIVAL OF THE TELEGRAPH

With changes in lifestyle came the need for a faster means of communication. People used to send messages via a rider who traveled by horse. This was a very slow method of communication.

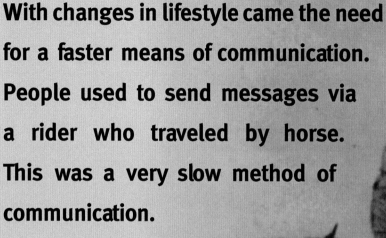

A Pony Express Rider, 1861

Morse key telegraph

The telegraph was about to change this as it would greatly increase the speed of communication. People who lived very far from each other would soon be able to send messages at what was once considered an unimaginable speed.

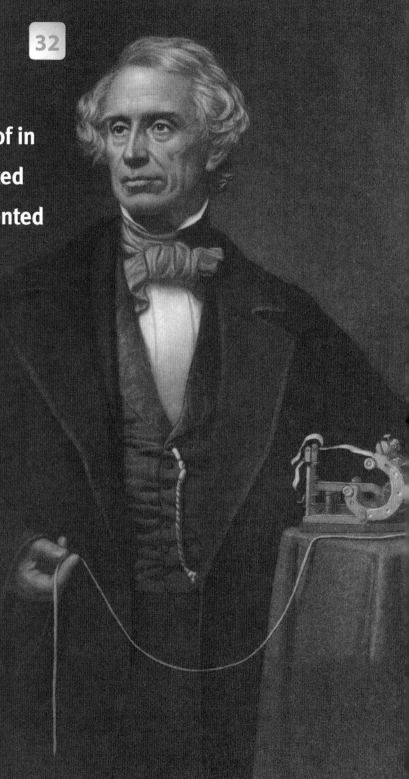

The telegraph was thought of in Britain as well as in the United States. The person who invented the telegraph in the United States was Samuel Morse. Morse was born in Charlestown, Massachusetts in 1871.

Samuel F. B. Morse

Although Morse enjoyed Art, after he enrolled in Yale University, he focused on Science courses. He graduated from university in 1810 and got a job in a publishing company.

Yale University, Connecticut, USA

He stayed in the publishing industry for roughly a year. Then he traveled to London, England to become involved in Art. While there, he was awarded a gold medal for one of the sculptures he created. When his art career did not turn out to be more fruitful, he went back to the United States. The year was 1815 and he turned his focus to painting portraits.

Morse traveled to London to pursue his art

In the many years that followed, Morse was involved in a variety of work. He was hired by New York University to teach Literature, Painting and Sculpturing.

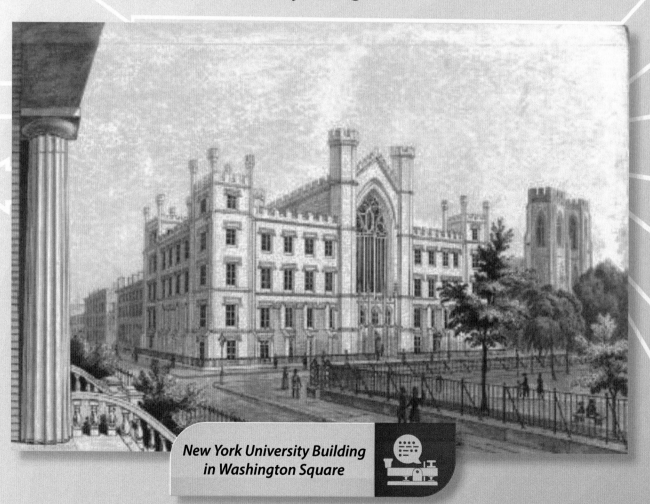

New York University Building in Washington Square

His interest in art also extended to the founding of the National Academy of Design. He even spent time in Europe. At one time, he decided to run for the position of mayor of New York City but he was not elected to this position.

Chapel of the Virgin at Subiaco, Samuel Morse Painting

In 1832, while he was employed as a painting teacher, he turned his focus on the possibility of transmitting messages on wire with the use of electricity. It was not until Morse had exhausted the idea of being a professional painter that he fully turned his attention to the areas of communication and

Morse in his workshop where he made his own instruments

This is when he started to work on the telegraph, a long-distance communication device in which messages are transmitted through wires with the use of electricity. The year 1837 was when he finally became devoted to inventing a telegraph.

Samuel F.B. Morse's first demonstration model of his telegraph was made with wooden canvas stretchers in 1837

Morse's telegraph was different from the telegraphs that were being used in Britain. In Britain, a telegraph relied on the use of several needles and wires.

A telegraph from Britain

With the help of Alfred Vail, Morse came up with a telegraph system that only needed one wire.

 Alfred Vail

He started out by using a metal plate to prevent electricity from flowing along a wire. He installed a key to the device to control the movements of the electrical currents. The flow of electricity was either opened or closed with the key. He then used a pencil that moved when electricity flowed through the wire.

A diagram of the Morse telegraph

Once the electrical current was stopped, the pencil wrote a message in the form of dots and dashes on a piece of paper. All of this enabled a message to be tapped out in what came to be called Morse Code.

Morse Telegraph (1837), historical collection of France Telecom

MORSE CODE

Morse Code is the system whereby letters, punctuation and numbers are represented by different symbols. These symbols include spaces, dots and dashes and they are arranged in a special way to transmit a message.

Morse Code

Letter	Code	Letter	Code	Letter	Code	Symbol	Code
A	·—	M	——	Y	—·——	6	—····
B	—···	N	—·	Z	——··	7	——···
C	—·—·	O	———	Ä	·—·—	8	———··
D	—··	P	·——·	Ö	———·	9	————·
E	·	Q	——·—	Ü	··——	.	·—·—·—
F	··—·	R	·—·	Ch	————	,	——··——
G	——·	S	···	0	—————	?	··——··
H	····	T	—	1	·————	!	··—·—·
I	··	U	··—	2	··———	:	———···
J	·———	V	···—	3	···——	"	·—··—·
K	—·—	W	·——	4	····—	'	·————·
L	·—··	X	—··—	5	·····	=	—···—

Once the key on the device is pressed, a message can be tapped out by using the different symbols. The symbols are changed into electrical signals that are transmitted along wire.

Morse Telegraph Key

When they are received by the telegraph to which they have been sent, they are changed back into a message. The Morse Code finally came together in 1838.

Morse System. Morse telegraph reciever

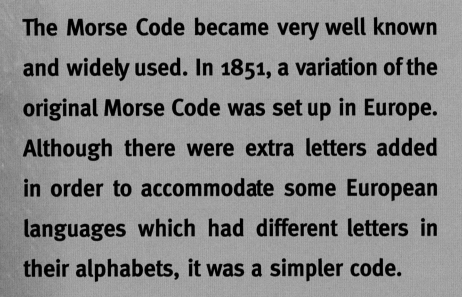

The Morse Code became very well known and widely used. In 1851, a variation of the original Morse Code was set up in Europe. Although there were extra letters added in order to accommodate some European languages which had different letters in their alphabets, it was a simpler code.

Samuel Morse and Telegraph

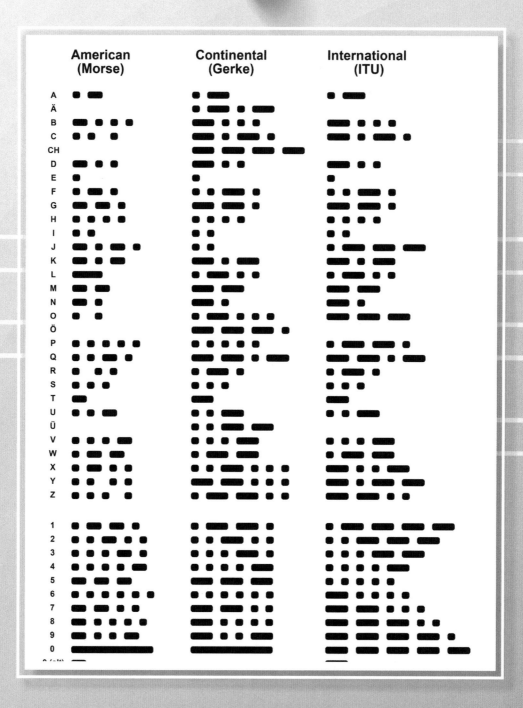

This modified version of the Morse Code went by two different names. Some people referred to it as the Continental Morse Code while others used the term, the International Morse Code. Either way, Morse's invention was helping to improve methods of long-distance communication.

Versions of Morse Code

THE EFFECTS OF THE TELEGRAPH

By transmitting a telegraph over a distance of 17,000 feet in 1837, Morse showed that his invention was a very fast and efficient means of long-distance communication.

Morse Telegraph Operator

He was issued a patent for his telegraph. The next thing that was needed was a long-distance line for the telegraph.

Morse "Port rule" transmitter. This is the first transmitter developed by Morse and Vail

This was seen to in 1843 when Morse was hired to build the line by the U.S. government. The line went from Washington, D.C. to Baltimore, Maryland. The first telegraph was transmitted the following year when the line was completed.

Samuel Morse sent the first public telegram on May 24, 1844. The message, "What Hath God Wrought!" was sent from the Supreme Court Chamber in the Capitol at Washington over a 40-mile wire to Baltimore

It was not too long before lines appeared all over the United States and Europe for the purpose of using telegraphs to communicate. In 1861, many countries in the world had lines. The age of fast communication had come.

 Two men hang telegraph wire

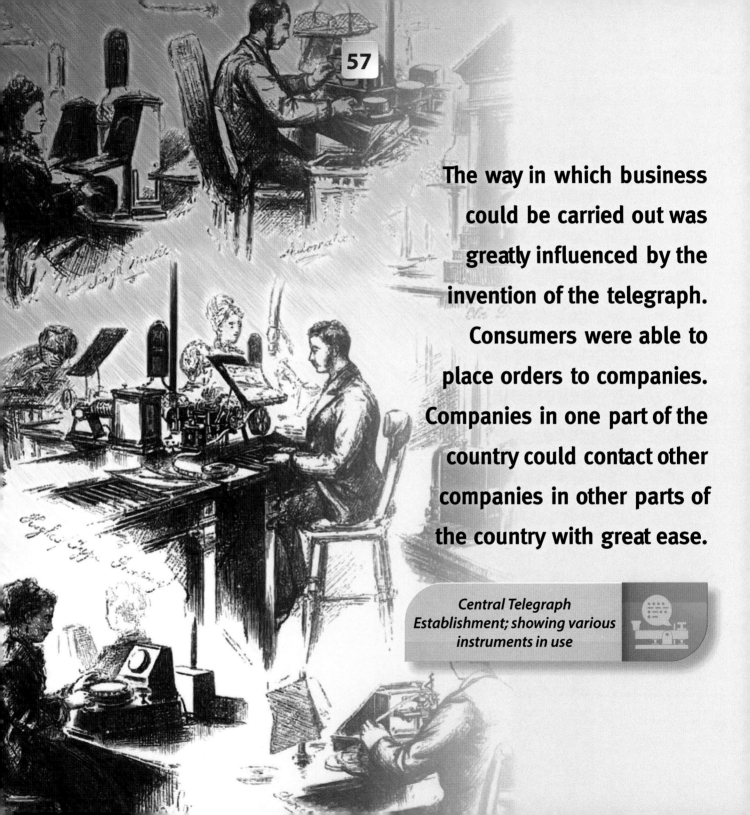

The way in which business could be carried out was greatly influenced by the invention of the telegraph. Consumers were able to place orders to companies. Companies in one part of the country could contact other companies in other parts of the country with great ease.

Central Telegraph Establishment; showing various instruments in use

Early forms of media, such as newspapers now had the advantage of a fast and reliable means to send out news. Even opportunities for international business were increased.

The Evening Telegraph.
May 15, 1865

Letter Carrier Delivering Mail

In addition to the effect on the economic growth of business, people's personal lifestyles started to change as a result of the use of the telegraph. At one time, people had to rely on the postal service to receive letters.

60

Now, in cases where fast communication was essential, people had the option of sending a telegraph. Moreover, people started to have faster access to news events and weather forecast.

Telegraph station on board ship for wireless telegraphy

Changes in the use of the telegraph started to be made in the first few years of the 1900s. In addition to relying on wires to transmit messages, improvements were made so that messages could also be transmitted via the air.

Woman sending message in Morse code

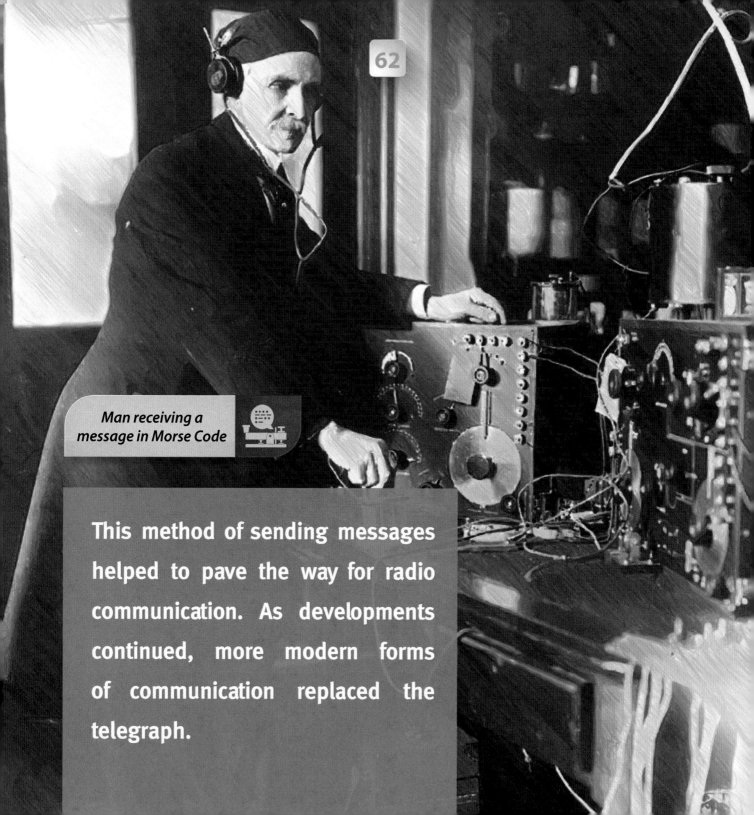

Man receiving a message in Morse Code

This method of sending messages helped to pave the way for radio communication. As developments continued, more modern forms of communication replaced the telegraph.

Vintage Computer from 1980

Around the end of the 20th Century, a new machine called a computer was starting to be used.

Morse became very wealthy as a result of his invention. He became a philanthropist who donated money to worthy causes. In addition to learning institutions, he made donations to churches and artists who were struggling financially.

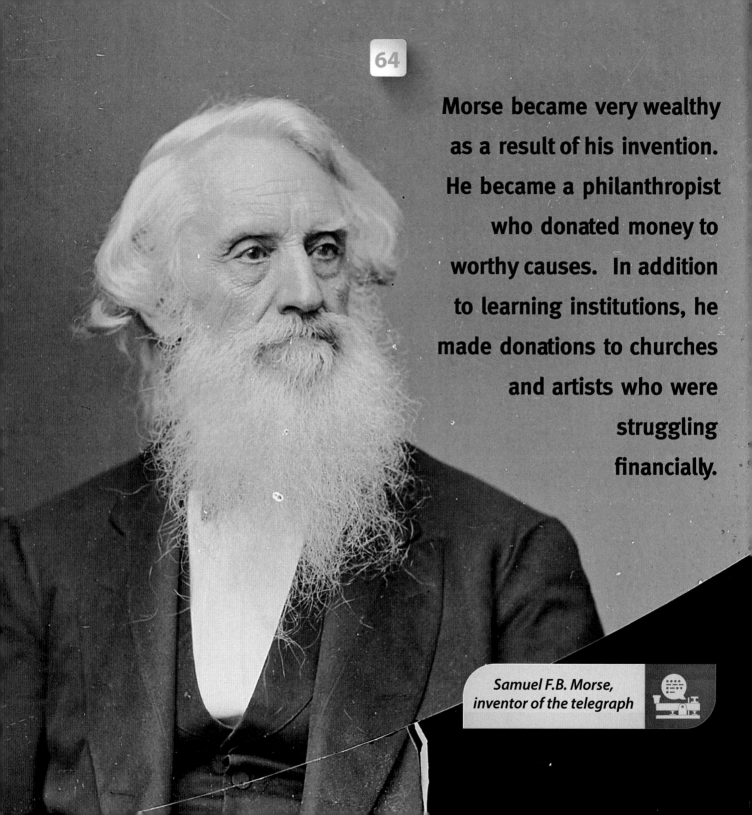

Samuel F.B. Morse, inventor of the telegraph

Locust Grove, a national historic site, not too far from Poughkeepsie, New York, was once owned by Morse.

Front of Locust Grove, located at 561 Blankenbaker Lane in Louisville, Kentucky, United States. Built in 1790, it is a National Historic Landmark

Morse died on April 2, 1872 in New York City.

Morse's telegraph strongly influenced communication. His invention changed how both people and companies communicated. After the telegraph, other inventions, such as the telephone, radio, televisions, computers and more recently the Internet have had a great impact on communication.

Woman sending Morse code using telegraph

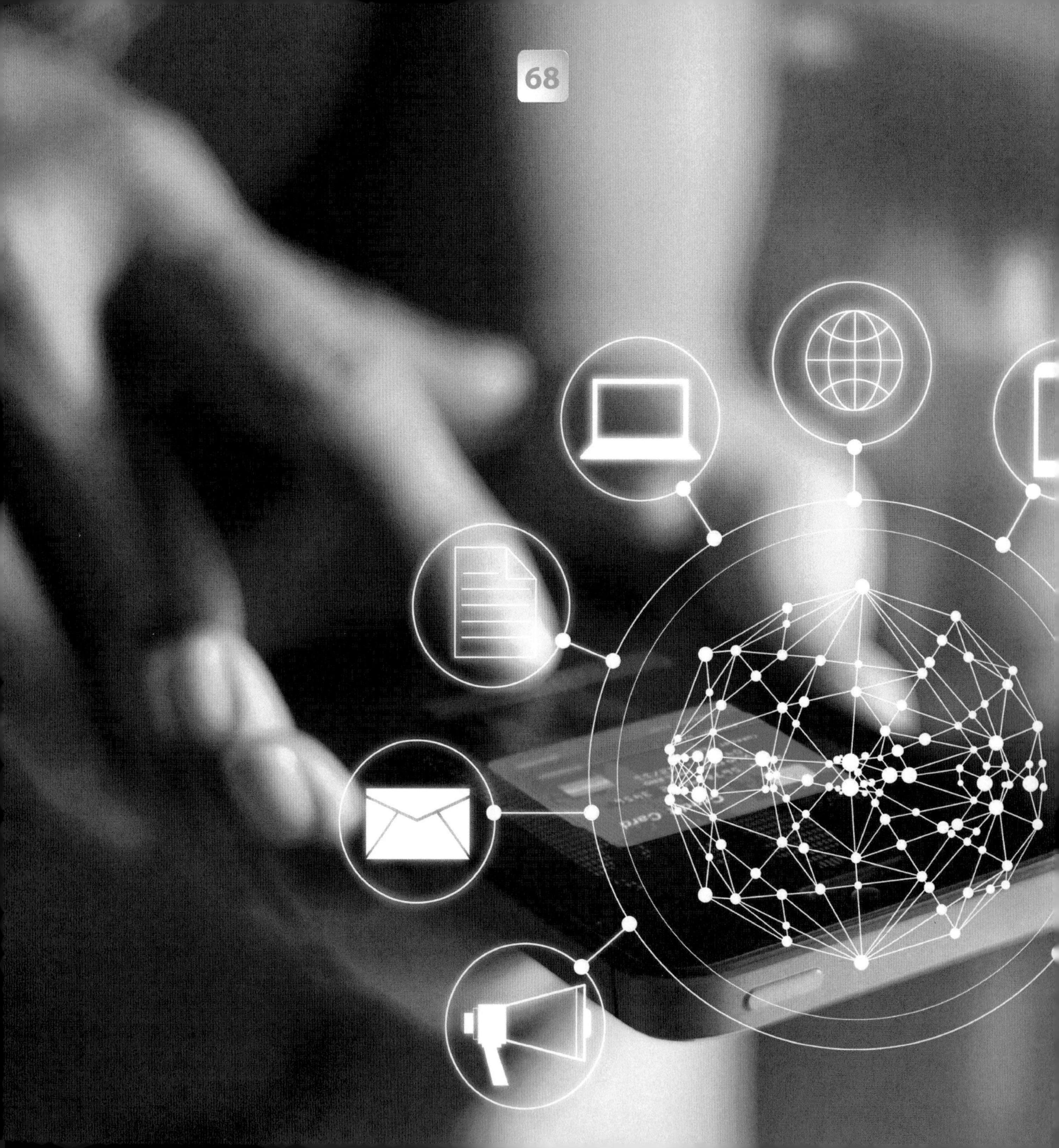

Today, almost everyone worldwide has access to mass media. Most people even own handheld devices through which long-distance communication can effortlessly be made.

A man using network connection on screen through his cellphone

Some of the inventions that allowed industries to flourish were the sewing machine, the reaper, the telegraph, and rubber. Learn about these inventions and other changes in the 1800s by reading more Baby Professor books.

Visit

BABY PROFESSOR
EDUCATION KIDS

www.speedypublishing.com

to download Free Baby Professor eBooks
and view our catalog of new and exciting
Children's Books

Made in the USA
Monee, IL
19 February 2021

60809125R00045